Lauren —
Be inspired.
Be authentic.
Be the best parent you can be — in this moment.

Duncan

Lauren —

Be inspired.
Be authentic.
Be the best person you
can be — in this
moment.

Trevor

Praise for Powerful Parenting

I love this book! It's a great reminder of how hard parenting can be and how taking a few moments to think can make it easier. It will inspire you to turn up with fun and joy so you can be the parent you want to be.

-*Dr. Orlena Kerek*

Being a parent is one of the hardest jobs in the world - especially considering we aren't provided with much training or support. It's important to take time to pause and reflect on all you have done and all you have to offer your children. This journal provides a wonderful opportunity to do that.

-*Lisa Niser*
Tax and Financial Advisor and Educator

So often we parents spend so much time doubting ourselves and doing the most for our families that we neglect replenishing ourselves. The affirmations in this journal provide space for us to breathe, reflect, and give ourselves much-needed grace. I plan to give this journal to friends as gifts. Thank you, Punam, for this incredible resource!

-*DeShanna Reed, Ed.D.*

You have a winner. The book reminds me of the inner voice pushing me forward and giving me praise and extra encouragement along the way.

-*Jessica Beck*
Teacher of the Gifted

The colorful, easy-to-read pages serve as bite-sized thought-provoking reminders and prompts for parents/caregivers to reflect on how we are showing up for our children. The first section focuses on the parent as a person by offering reminders to take care of ourselves. The second section reminds us to reflect on how we are guiding, leading, and role-modeling as parents. And in the last section, the quotes gently remind parents/caregivers that we have the tremendous responsibility to enforce boundaries and to empower children to meet expectations. As a mom, aunt, and teacher, I need these reminders often to bring me back to what's really important.

-*Crystal Frommert*
Math Educator
Author, When Calling Parents isn't Your Calling

Whatever your parenting journey looks like--solo, coupled, rooted in your village-- Powerful Parenting reminds us to pause and reflect on the journey. So many parenting books are prescriptive, but the beauty of Powerful Parenting is that this book reminds us to extend grace to ourselves and take a moment to realize that we are doing our best even if our journeys are different from our friends and neighbors.

-*Tracy Harbin*
Honors Director
Seminole State College, Florida

Praise for Powerful Parenting

I love this book! It's a great reminder of how hard parenting can be and how taking a few moments to think can make it easier. It will inspire you to turn up with fun and joy so you can be the parent you want to be.

-Dr. Orlena Kerek

Being a parent is one of the hardest jobs in the world - especially considering we aren't provided with much training or support. It's important to take time to pause and reflect on all you have done and all you have to offer your children. This journal provides a wonderful opportunity to do that.

-Lisa Niser
Tax and Financial Advisor and Educator

So often we parents spend so much time doubting ourselves and doing the most for our families that we neglect replenishing ourselves. The affirmations in this journal provide space for us to breathe, reflect, and give ourselves much-needed grace. I plan to give this journal to friends as gifts. Thank you, Punam, for this incredible resource!

-DeShanna Reed, Ed.D.

You have a winner. The book reminds me of the inner voice pushing me forward and giving me praise and extra encouragement along the way.

-Jessica Beck
Teacher of the Gifted

The colorful, easy-to-read pages serve as bite-sized thought-provoking reminders and prompts for parents/caregivers to reflect on how we are showing up for our children. The first section focuses on the parent as a person by offering reminders to take care of ourselves. The second section reminds us to reflect on how we are guiding, leading, and role-modeling as parents. And in the last section, the quotes gently remind parents/caregivers that we have the tremendous responsibility to enforce boundaries and to empower children to meet expectations. As a mom, aunt, and teacher, I need these reminders often to bring me back to what's really important.

-Crystal Frommert
Math Educator
Author, When Calling Parents isn't Your Calling

Whatever your parenting journey looks like--solo, coupled, rooted in your village-- Powerful Parenting reminds us to pause and reflect on the journey. So many parenting books are prescriptive, but the beauty of Powerful Parenting is that this book reminds us to extend grace to ourselves and take a moment to realize that we are doing our best even if our journeys are different from our friends and neighbors.

-Tracy Harbin
Honors Director
Seminole State College, Florida

Powerful Parenting: 101 Ways to Stay Positive

A Parent Affirmation Journal

Punam V. Saxena, M.Ed.

This book is written from the author's personal experiences.
Any likeness or similarities to other works are coincidences.

Copyright © 2023 by Punam V. Saxena

All rights reserved. Published by edu-Me, LLC

No part of this book may be reproduced or used in any manner without written permission of the copyright owner except for the use of quotations in a book review. For more information, address: punamvsaxena@gmail.com.

Library of Congress Control Number: 2023915376

First edition September 2023

Cover design by Punam V. Saxena

ISBN 978-1-7366402-4-1 (paperback)

www.punamvsaxena.com

*To my husband, who is the stronger,
more patient parent, never wavering in
his love and support*

*To my children, who make me a better
human and want to strive for more*

*To my parents, from whom I've learned
the importance of family*

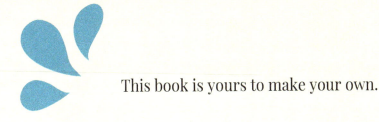

This book is yours to make your own.

The quotes in this book are meant to be thought-provoking and reflective. After reading the quote, you can journal your thoughts.

If a quote does not align with your family's values, simply move on.

This book is not about judgment but about reaffirming your capabilities as an amazing parent*.

This book is an opportunity to reflect on your parenting, validate yourself, and allow yourself permission to acknowledge the parent you are now and the one you would like to become.

In solidarity,

Punam

*"Parents" is used in this book to describe all caregivers, concerned persons, and advocates for children.

This book is yours to make your own.

The quotes in this book are meant to be thought-provoking and reflective. After reading the quote, you can journal your thoughts.

If a quote does not align with your family's values, simply move on.

This book is not about judgment but about reaffirming your capabilities as an amazing parent*.

This book is an opportunity to reflect on your parenting, validate yourself, and allow yourself permission to acknowledge the parent you are now and the one you would like to become.

In solidarity,

Punam

"Parents" is used in this book to describe all caregivers, concerned persons, and advocates for children.

For YOU

Love is the best four-letter word in the English language. Use it often.

What's your favorite word?

Remember to breathe.

How do you relax?

Stay true to your beliefs, regardless of what others say.

What values are you not willing to change?

Do one thing for yourself every day, even if it's for 15 minutes.

What did you do for your 15 minutes?

Laugh at yourself. It's healthy for your mind and spirit.

What made you laugh today?

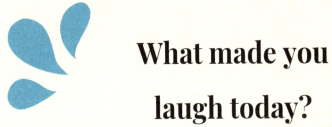

Find a trustworthy support person to share confidential information—a therapist, friend, significant other, or family member.

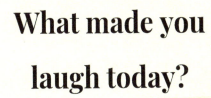

What made you laugh today?

Find a trustworthy support person to share confidential information—a therapist, friend, significant other, or family member.

Who's on your list?

Celebrate your accomplishments, not what is still on your to-do list. Your smallest accomplishments are wins!

What was today's win?

Need a break? Take it!

Take the break!

Parenting is an exhausting and most rewarding job.

What exhausted you?
What relaxed you?

You are doing the best you can at this moment in time. Be OK with that.

You are THE best!

Thank goodness for UberEats and DoorDash. Some days, you've earned it!

No cooking required!
Yay!

Dream big. Your dreams are important, too.

What's your big dream?

Encourage your children to think outside the box. The best innovations occur when we think big.

Be creative!

Be mindful of your schedule: under-commit and over-deliver. You'll come out a hero!

What did you do to be a hero today?

Every day is a new opportunity to create beautiful memories with your children.

What memories did you make today?

Some days are just rough. Acknowledge it and start again tomorrow.

Find a group of fellow parents who are encouraging and supportive.

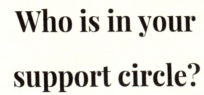

Who is in your support circle?

You're tired. You're exhausted. It's ok, but never give up!

Keep moving, even it's baby steps.

It is essential to take care of yourself, so you can better care for your children. What will you do for yourself today?

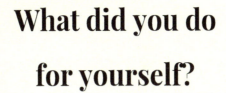

What did you do for yourself?

Do something outside your comfort zone that is exhilarating and exciting. Be Safe!

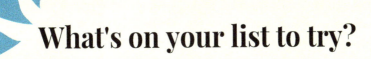

What's on your list to try?

Give yourself a parent time-out when it's overwhelming. We all need a breather.

Where did you go for your time-out?

For You, the Parent

Raising children is a journey best traveled with laughter and ice cream.

What's your favorite ice cream flavor?

Love and support your children unconditionally.

How do you express love to your children?

Every relationship is built on trust and confidence. Be trustworthy and instill confidence in your children. They need to know you have their back.

What can you do to instill confidence in your children?

Create family activities that become traditions.

What activities do you all enjoy together?

Create a family book club. Enjoy snacks and sparkling grape juice as you reflect on the book.

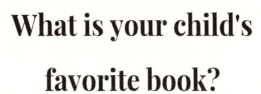

What is your child's favorite book?

Laugh with your children every day.

Be the role model your child needs.

Better you than someone else.

Who is your role model?

Patience may be a virtue
but patience with children
deserves a halo.

Always, *always* be proud of your child.

How does your child make you proud?

Know when your child needs a hug.

Discuss a variety of topics in your home, so your children know that they can, too.

What topics do you discuss with your child?

Value your relationship with your children, just like your other relationships.

How do you value your relationships?

Apologize for your mistakes. Children will learn to acknowledge theirs, too.

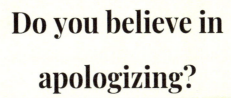

Do you believe in apologizing?

Set up a weekly calendar for the family that includes everyone's obligations and place it prominently, so everyone knows the schedule.

Do you prefer a digital or paper calendar?

Plan your family's daily activities so you will be prepared when emergencies occur.

Are you a planner or a free-thinker?

Parenting is hard. There is no manual. The only thing they need to know you love them.

How do you show your child love?

Frustration and exhaustion are a part of parenting. Acknowledge it, tell your children, and give yourself grace.

How do you give yourself grace?

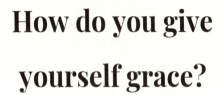

Every birthday is a gift. Make your child's day special.

How do you celebrate birthdays?

The only thing children need is your love.

Talk *with* your children, not at them.

How can you start a conversation with your child?

Want to know what's happening in their lives? Tell them what's happening in yours.

What's happening in your life that you can share?

For You, the Parent at School

Try to send your children to school with a smile on their face. Positive feelings from home create positive feelings at school.

-My Mom

This is not always possible, but we can try.

You are the most valuable advocate for your child. Use your voice wisely and trust your gut.

How do you advocate for your child?

Be the parent teachers and administrators are happy to see walk through the door.

How do you interact with teachers and administrators?

When discussing your children's school and teacher, speak positively. Children will respond the same.

How can you speak positively about the school?

Your children's mental health is more important than their grades. (Although grades ARE important.)

Is your child in a healthy space?

Parents are the key to their child's academic success. Engage with their teachers and build a relationship because children need a support team.

Engaging in school does not require in-person meetings. Emails and phone calls can be as successful.

Be the parent who brings a smile to another child. It may be the only smile they see all day.

How did your smile make a difference?

Get involved in the school's parent organization, even if it's for one hour a year. There is nothing better than a caring school volunteer.

Does your schedule allow you to commit to volunteering?

Is your child having trouble at school? Listen to their teacher's point of view before chastising them. Then work to find a solution together.

What kind of listener are you?

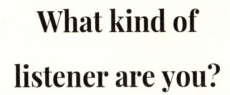

Let your child's teacher know their positive impact on your child.

How does the teacher positively impact your child?

Help your child's teacher by volunteering however you are able.

Be realistic and content with your volunteering. No judgment.

Your children seeing you in school lets them know you care.

How do you feel when you see your child during the school day?

A trade school is just as valuable as a college degree. Encourage children to chase their passions, not accolades.

What's your child's passion?

Resolve conflicts at school with respect, thoughtfulness, and optimism.

How do you resolve conflicts?

Remember, you've given your children the tools to fly after high school. However, let them know you are there to catch them if they need it.

Your children are ready.

Are you?

For You, the Teacher

Communicate, communicate, communicate to prevent misunderstandings.

Kindness, compassion, and empathy create life-long relationships.
Be sure to teach your child these skills.

How are you teaching your child empathy?

You don't always have to like your child's choices, but you do need to support them every day.

In what ways do you support your child's choices?

Be punctual for your children's activities. They want to see you value their activities by being on time.

Put it on your calendar and schedule it like any other appointment.

Children need "safe fails." We all do. Let them try new activities in the safety of your home where there is support and positive affirmation.

In what areas do you allow 'safe fails' for your children?

Tell your child when you don't know something. It's an opportunity to grow and learn together.

What has your child taught you?

Children remember the highs and lows of their childhood. Make the highs overshadow the lows.

What would you like them to remember about their childhood?

Share your accomplishments with your children. They want to cheer for you, too!

What are your accomplishments?

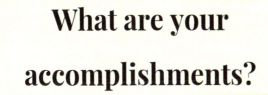

There is a time to give advice to your children and a time to listen.

Do you listen to your child?

Look for small behavior changes in your child. They could be a sign of a more significant issue that needs to be addressed.

Do you see any changes in your child's behavior?

Don't be afraid to be the parent in the room. Sometimes, that's exactly what children need.

How do you parent your child?

Children are always listening, whether they look like it or not. Be watchful of what you say.

Has your child heard something you wished they had not?*

*Mine have. It can be tough to navigate those situations.

Be the parent your child needs right now.

YES!

Never criticize or yell at your children in public. If their behavior needs to be addressed, whisper in their ear. It's a win-win for everyone!

Could this work for you?

Let children advise you on some issues so they consider your advice when you share yours.

What advice have your children given that worked for you?

Have an open conversation about social justice issues occurring today. Make sure you listen to your child's perspective, even if you disagree.

What social justice issues impact you and your family?

A clean house is a pipe dream. Your children will not remember your museum-clean house. They will remember the painting activity, icing all over the kitchen, and the blanket tent in the family room. A clean home can happen when they're off and independent (or not!).

Make the mess! It's worth it.
(Even if you need to clean up afterward.)

Be "THE" house where your children want their friends over. It's a great way to know who they are hanging out with.

Whose house do your children hang out in?

Fiercely guard your child's privacy. Everyone does not need to know everything.

How do you protect your child's privacy?

**Be firm in
non-negotiable situations.
Let the rest go.**

What is non-negotiable for you?

Children are finding their voice and need a safe, nonjudgmental place to share their thoughts.

How do you react when your child shares their feelings?

Want motivated children? Show them your motivation first. Theirs will follow.

What motivates you?

Children will put away their shoes or bring their dishes to the sink when you expect them to (and when you do!). Gentle reminders will, eventually, become habits.

What habits would you like to instill in your child?

Respect your children's privacy, as is age appropriate. They need a bit of agency over themselves.

How do you offer independence to your child?

Children are born curious. Your job is to make sure they never lose it.

What can you do to make sure your child stays curious?

When you expect more for your children, they will work hard to reach it.

What are your expectations?

Encourage your child's creativity, like art, music, or dance. A well-rounded child grows into a well-rounded adult.

What is your child's creative outlet?

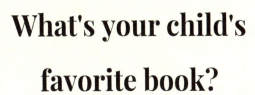

What's your child's favorite book?

Teach your child the importance of prioritizing their responsibilities.

What's important?
What can be done later?

Teach your child to own their mistakes. It's a sign of strength.

Do you own your mistakes?

Encourage a strong work ethic at school and work. Hard work is a recognized and valued trait.

Do you consider yourself a hard worker? How does it help you?

Social media rules: Make them with your children, so you have buy-in from them.

What are some social media rules in your house?

Teach your child how to receive feedback so they can learn, reflect, and expand their understanding of the world.

How does your child receive feedback?

Teach your child how to give feedback in a constructive manner.

What can you do to help your child share their feedback?

Teach children the value of working hard and fiscal responsibility.

Does your child understand the value of finances?

Teach your children to use social media in a safe and healthy way.

What social media apps do you allow your child to use?

Teach your children to write "Thank You" notes. Acknowledging another person's kindness is a necessary skill.

What is your method for acknowledging someone else's kindness?

Teach your child to cook at least three meals so they can be self-sufficient in the kitchen.

What are your child's favorite meals that they can learn to cook?

Teach your children to enjoy what they have. There is no shortage of "stuff" to buy, but being content is critical to happiness.

How much "stuff" is enough?

Teach your child not to be wasteful of food and money. Both are precious resources.

How are you teaching these values?

Pat yourself on the back.
You are doing a GREAT job!
Your children are fortunate and grateful.

If no one else tells you, I am. You are doing an amazing job and I'm so proud of you for working hard, raising your children, and creating kind citizens of our society.
Be proud of yourself!

Punam

About the Author

Punam V. Saxena holds a B.A. in Psychology and an M.Ed. in Education and is working on her doctorate. Throughout her 30 years of teaching and volunteering in her children's schools, she implemented several procedures that have benefited the students and administrators within the school district.

She is a Parent Impact Coach, TEDx and SXSW speaker, podcast host of edu-Me, and a published author. She focuses on bridging the gap and fostering stronger relationships between parents and schools by empowering parents to become partners in their child's education. Her passion and work stem from her life experiences as a first-generation Indian American and raising her own four children.

Punam has been featured on NBC's Atlanta & Company, CBS, ABC, FOX, and several magazine articles.

For professional development and coaching, send an email to punamvsaxena@gmail.com.

Printed in the USA
CPSIA information can be obtained
at www.ICGtesting.com
JSHW010756170923
48403JS00001B/1